The Outer Planets

RUTH ASHBY

Published by Smart Apple Media, 1980 Lookout Drive, North Mankato, Minnesota 56003

Photo credits: Page 4: courtesy NASA/JPL/California Institute of Technology. Page 5: copyright © 2003 Mansell. Page 7: courtesy NASA. Page 8: courtesy NASA/JPL/University of Arizona. Page 10: copyright © 2003 Calvin J. Hamilton. Page 11 (top): courtesy NASA JPL. Page 11 (bottom), 12: courtesy NASA. Page 13: courtesy Voyager 2/NASA Page 14 (top): courtesy Voyager1/NASA/JPL. Page 14 (bottom), 15, 16: courtesy NASA. Page 17: copyright © 2003 Calvin J. Hamilton. Page 19: courtesy NASA. Page 20: courtesy Astronomical Society of the Pacific. Page 21: courtesy NASA/JPL/Dave Seal. Page 23: courtesy NASA/JPL/TIMEPIX. Page 24: courtesy NASA/JPL. Page 25: copyright © 2003 Calvin J. Hamilton. Page 26, 27: courtesy NASA. Page 29: copyright © 2003 Calvin J. Hamilton. Page 30: courtesy NASA. Page 32: copyright © 2003 Calvin J. Hamilton. Page 33, 34, 35, 36, 37, 38: courtesy NASA. Page 41: courtesy Pat Rawlings/NASA/JPL. Page 42: courtesy Gemini Observatory/NOAO/AURA/NSF. Page 44 (top): courtesy NASA/JPL/University of Arizona. Page 44 (bottom): courtesy NASA. Page 45 (top): courtesy NASA/JPL. Page 45 (middle), 45 (bottom): courtesy NASA.
Cover art © 2003 Chris Butler.

Library of Congress Cataloging-in-Publication Data

Ashby, Ruth.
The outer planets / by Ruth Ashby.
p. cm. — (The new solar system)
Summary: A discussion of the planets Jupiter, Saturn, Uranus, Neptune, and Pluto, and how to observe them. Includes index.
ISBN 1-58340-290-X
1. Outer planets—Juvenile literature. [1. Planets.] I. Title. II. Series.
QB639.A78 2003   523.4—dc21   2003045487

First Edition

9 8 7 6 5 4 3 2 1

Contents

These photographs of Jupiter and its four largest, or Galilean, moons were taken by *Voyager I* and assembled into this collage. Although the moons are not to scale, they are in their correct positions relative to Jupiter. Clockwise from Jupiter, they are Callisto, Ganymede, Europa, and Io.

Origin of the Outer Planets

In August 1609, Italian scientist Galileo Galilei fashioned a telescope, aimed it at the sky, and made history. The telescope had been invented by a Dutch eyeglass maker the previous year; however, Galileo was the first to use it to study the heavens. The marvels he witnessed had never been seen by human eyes. He saw mountains, craters, valleys on the Moon, and countless stars in the Milky Way. On January 7, 1610, he made the most amazing discovery of all. The planet Jupiter had four orbiting bodies, or moons. Overwhelmed, Galileo wrote, "I am filled with amazement and offer unending thanks to God that it has pleased Him to reveal through me such great wonders, unknown to all the centuries before our time."

With his observations of Venus, Jupiter, and Saturn, Galileo invented planetary science. Ancient observers had distinguished between stars and planets but were forced to rely on the power of their unaided eyes. They noticed that the stars remained in fixed patterns that circled in a great band across the dome of the heavens. They also noticed seven bodies moving among the stars: the Sun, the Moon, and five others. The Greeks called these five others "planets," or wanderers, and named them after the Greek gods Hermes, Aphrodite, Ares, Zeus, and Cronos. Today we know them by their Roman names: Mercury, Venus, Mars, Jupiter, and Saturn. In the four centuries since Galileo's time, we have discovered three more: Uranus, Neptune, and Pluto.

In 1609, Galileo presented one of his first telescopes to the Doge (chief magistrate) of Venice. He demonstrated that, using the telescope, one could see the flags of distant ships entering the harbor.

For most of human history, the planets were mysterious objects in an endless sky, unreachable and unknowable. In the past 100 years, we have discovered more about them than in the previous 5,000. We have sent men to the Moon and launched spacecraft to explore the solar system. We now know planets as more than just the stuff of science fiction. They are complicated, three-dimensional worlds—beautiful yet mysterious.

Our solar system was born about 4.6 billion years ago in a spiral galaxy called the Milky Way. A nebula, or great cloud of gas and dust, began to contract until it reached a mass about 1,200 times that of the largest planet, Jupiter. A temperature of 10 million K, or 18 million°F (10 million°C), triggered nuclear fusion, and our Sun "turned on." Dust from the nebula swirled about the Sun, colliding, then merging together, and eventually becoming large chunks called "planetesimals." As these clumps grew, so did their gravitational pull, until most of the dust had collected into the nine bodies we now know as the planets. The solar wind blew most of the lighter gas to the outer planets, where it formed the gas giants Jupiter, Saturn, Uranus, and Neptune. The four innermost, or terrestrial planets—Mercury, Venus, Earth, and Mars—remained rocky, composed of heavier metals.

The orbits of the first eight planets and their moons are all on roughly the same plane, called the "ecliptic." Pluto, the ninth planet, is the exception. Its orbit typically deviates from the ecliptic by 17.2 degrees. All of the planets move around the Sun in the same direction: counterclockwise. The solar system is so huge—almost 11 trillion miles (17.7 trillion km) from one boundary to the other—that even though the four inner planets are relatively close to the Sun, they're still unimaginably far away.

Voyager to the Stars

The most distant artificial objects in the universe are more than seven billion miles (12 billion km) away. When *Voyager 1* and *Voyager 2* completed their mission in 1989, they continued their flight away from Earth. Both were headed out of the solar system and into the heliosphere, the region where interstellar space begins. The *Voyagers* travel too far from the Sun to use solar panels. They are powered by devices called "radioisotope thermoelectric generators" (RTGs). These convert heat from the natural radioactive decay of plutonium into electricity to power the spacecraft instruments, computers and other systems. Until the year 2020, instruments on board the spacecraft will continue to return data about the Sun's magnetic field, the solar wind, and cosmic rays. Then, the *Voyager* spacecraft will lose power and drift among the stars for eternity.

The start of solar system exploration was one of the triumphs of the late 20th century. For the past four decades, the National Aeronautics and Space Administration, more commonly known as NASA, has sent robotic spacecraft to explore the planets of the solar system and the interplanetary environment. These spacecraft communicate with Earth via radio waves, which travel at the speed of light. In the 1970s, *Pioneer 10* and *11* became the first human-made objects to fly by Jupiter and Saturn and observe the huge planets at close range.

In 1977, NASA's *Voyager* spacecraft began a grand tour of the outer planets. *Voyager 1* traveled to Jupiter and Saturn and returned the kind of data and images that earlier generations of scientists had only dreamed about. Building on their success, scientists sent *Voyager 2* on a planet-hopping expedition from Jupiter and Saturn out to Uranus and Neptune. *Voyager 2* used the gravitational force of one planet to go to the next, a method called "gravity assist."

The triumphant *Pioneer* and *Voyager* missions and the *Galileo* mission that followed revolutionized our understanding of the outer planets. What we now know about these fantastic gas giants we owe to these missions and to the men and women who made their dream of space exploration a reality.

In August 1989, the *Galileo* spacecraft was installed into the payload bay of the space shuttle *Atlantis* at the Kennedy Space Center. It rode into space on the shuttle before being launched on its mission to Jupiter.

This true-color view of Jupiter is composed of four images taken by NASA's *Cassini* spacecraft on December 7, 2000.

CHAPTER ONE

Jupiter: The Giant Among Us

Jupiter is the biggest planet in the solar system. It is 89,000 miles (143,000 km) in diameter—11 times wider than Earth. If Jupiter were hollow, it could swallow more than 1,300 Earths. In fact, it weighs more than twice as much as all of the other planets put together. Jupiter is so gigantic it could swallow up the rest of the planets and materials in the solar system, excluding the Sun.

Even though it is almost 390 million miles (630 million km) from Earth, Jupiter lights up the sky—it's the second-brightest planet in the night sky, after Venus. It's no wonder that the ancient Romans named it Jupiter after the king of the gods, the Lord of Heaven.

Jupiter has a highly elliptical, or oval, orbit. At perihelion, the point in its path when it's closest to the Sun, it orbits at a distance of 460 million miles (740 million km). At aphelion, the point in its path when it is farthest from the Sun, it is nearly 50 million miles (80 million km) farther away. Because Jupiter is so remote, it takes 11.9 of our years to make one complete revolution around the Sun. But its rotation on its axis is the fastest of all the planets, clocking in at approximately 9 hours and 50 minutes, which makes Earth's 24-hour rotation seem relatively lazy. Spinning so swiftly causes Jupiter to flatten at its poles and bulge ever so slightly at its equator.

Jupiter is composed primarily of the two most common elements in the solar system, hydrogen and helium, with traces of ammonia, methane, and water vapor. Its core is rocky and about 10 to 15 times the mass of Earth, with a diameter of about 7,500 miles (12,000 km). The core is composed mostly of metals and silicon, and its temperature is hotter than the surface of the Sun—an unbelievable 36,000°F (20,000°C). Above the core is the mantle, which extends about 12,500 miles (20,000 km). There the pressure is so great and the temperature so scaldingly hot that hydrogen gas turns into metallic hydrogen. Above the mantle, there is a level of liquid hydrogen and, finally, hydrogen gas.

Because Jupiter's mass is so great and its gravitational pull is so strong, it acts like a humongous vacuum cleaner for the solar system. Most comets and asteroids don't reach the inner planets because they're sucked into Jupiter's orbit. In this way, Jupiter acts as a giant bodyguard for Earth.

Recently, astronomers got to see the bodyguard in action for the first time. In March 1993, they tracked pieces of a comet that had been pulled apart by Jupiter's gravitational forces. In July 1994, this comet, named Shoemaker-Levy 9, crashed into Jupiter at 130,000 miles (210,000 km) per hour, leaving dark scars in the giant planet's cloud bands. Some of the impact craters were as large as Earth.

Because Jupiter's inner layer of metallic hydrogen conducts electricity, it generates the strongest magnetic field of all the planets, 2,000 times greater than Earth's. Its magnetosphere, the magnetized envelope around the planet, extends millions of miles into space. Charged particles from the Sun's solar wind and from Io, one of Jupiter's moons, enter the magnetosphere to form an intense radiation belt. Space probes that visit Jupiter have to be equipped with special shields to protect against damage by radiation bombardment.

The surface of Jupiter is shrouded in a thick atmosphere some 600 miles (966 km) deep. The atmosphere is composed

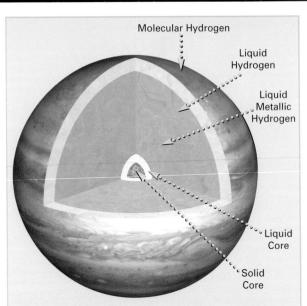

The surface layer of Jupiter is hydrogen gas. Below it, the planet's mantle is composed of liquid hydrogen. As it descends to the core, the mantle changes to liquid metallic hydrogen due to heat and pressure. The core itself has two components: a smaller, inner, rocky core, and a liquid core surrounding it composed of water, methane, and ammonia ice.

The Great Dark Spot?

Is the Great Red Spot the largest feature on Jupiter? Recent images from the *Cassini* spacecraft suggest that there's something even bigger—the Great Dark Spot. In 2000, as *Cassini* flew by Jupiter on its way to Saturn, its ultraviolet cameras picked up a dark oval shape on the planet's north pole. Apparently, the Great Dark Spot is caused by high-energy electrons from Jupiter's magnetic field hitting its upper atmosphere. The Spot is not visible all the time, and can be seen only in ultraviolet light.

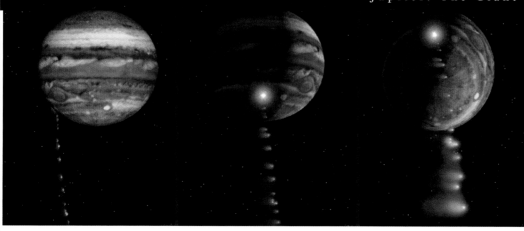

This series of illustrations, from three different perspectives, depicts the comet Shoemaker-Levy 9 colliding with Jupiter.

of approximately 86 percent hydrogen, 13.8 percent helium, and traces of other chemicals such as methane, ammonia, and water vapor. The whitish clouds of ammonia crystals circulating in the top layer are about ⁻190°F (⁻120°C). Beneath them are dark-orange bands of ammonium hydrosulfide, and beneath them, bluish clouds of water ice. It's probably the sulfur and additional phosphorus compounds that explain in part the planet's Technicolor brilliance.

Jupiter's rapid rotation causes the atmospheric clouds to be pulled into different-colored bands. The light bands, called "zones," result from gas shooting up from the warm interior and then condensing. The dark bands, called "belts," mark the layers of cold, descending gas. Within different zones and belts, winds blow in alternating directions at speeds of up to 400 miles (600 km) per hour. Sometimes huge lightning bolts flash across the clouds.

This turbulent atmosphere is also evident in the planet's many eddying storms. The largest and most well-known is called the Great Red Spot. This

Voyager 1 took this picture of the Great Red Spot, the largest hurricane in the solar system. Jupiter's atmosphere is a violent world of eddying storms and currents.

11

immense storm system was first noted in 1664, when astronomer Robert Hooke spotted it in his telescope. The storm, which towers five miles (8 km) above the surrounding clouds, varies in color, going from bright red to a much duller hue. Its size varies as well, as it is sometimes as large as three Earths and other times only as large as one. It is not known why the storm has lasted so long.

As befits such a giant, Jupiter is at the center of its own miniature planetary system. It has 61 known moons, ranging from more than 3,000 miles (5,200 km) in diameter to 1 mile (1.6 km). The inner eight have circular orbits in the plane of the planet's equator; the others are elliptical. We know the most about the four largest moons, which were discovered by Galileo and are known, fittingly, as the "Galilean moons." Named after the god Jupiter's most famous mythological lovers—Io, Europa, Ganymede, and Callisto—they are some of the most fascinating objects in the solar system.

Io

On March 9, 1979, *Voyager 2* sent back one of the most unexpected and exciting images of its journey: Io, the Galilean moon closest to Jupiter, was erupting, spewing hot sulfur nearly 200 miles (322 km) into space. With nine known live volcanoes, Io is the most volcanically active body in the entire solar system. So much lava is ejected yearly—11 billion tons (10 billion t)—that Io's surface is always being reshaped. The lava covers and smoothes over any craters left by crashing meteors. As a result, Io is a blotchy, orange-red body with bulging black blemishes. As one scientist put it when he first glimpsed Io, "I've seen better-looking pizza."

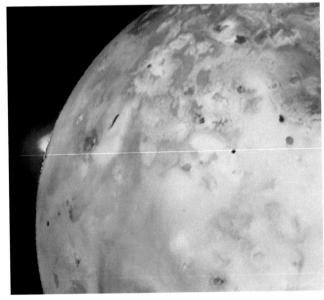

The distinctive yellow-orange color of Jupiter's moon Io comes from the sulfur belched out by its many active volcanoes. In this image taken by the *Voyager 1* spacecraft, the plume of the volcano Loki can be seen on the edge.

What causes all of that volcanic activity on Io? It's due to the combined gravitational pulls of Jupiter and two of its other moons, Europa and Ganymede. Because Io is so close to its parent planet—it orbits at only 262,300 miles (421,600 km) away—Jupiter exerts a strong pull on Io called a "tidal force." In addition, Io passes close to Europa on every other orbit and close to Ganymede on every fourth orbit. The interaction between the three gravitational forces causes Io's crust to flex and its interior to melt.

Europa

Europa has a bright reflective surface composed of water ice, giving it the smoothest appearance of any body in the solar system. However, a network of dark lines crisscrosses the ice, making the moon look like a cracked egg. Although Europa is farther from Jupiter than Io—417,000 miles (670,000 km)—it, too, is affected by tidal gravitational forces. And perhaps the cracks are caused by water from the interior heating up and pushing through the ice crust.

Scientists suspect that beneath the ice might be an ocean of slushy water, with a hard rocky core at the center. Readings of the moon's spectra taken by the *Galileo* spacecraft in 1997 revealed that there may be some carbon-containing material along the ice cracks. Carbon is the element on which all life on Earth is based. Some scientists dare to dream that Europa's icy seas contain microscopic life-forms.

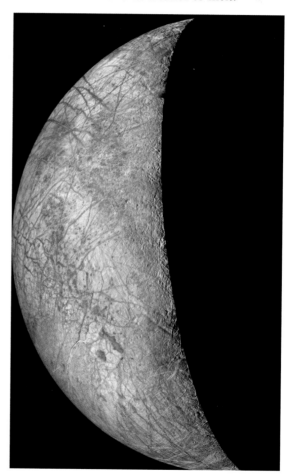

This image of the crescent moon Europa was captured by *Voyager 2* in 1979. About the same size as—but much smoother than—Earth's Moon, Europa has a surface of cracked ice. Evidence exists to indicate that liquid oceans might be hidden beneath Europa's icy shell.

Ganymede

Ganymede is the largest of Jupiter's Galilean moons; in fact, it is the largest moon in the solar system. At 3,269 miles (5,260 km) in diameter, it is even larger than Mercury. Patterns of dark and light play along its surface—dark, ancient rock and ice and lighter, more recently developed areas of ice. The dark areas are pockmarked with impact craters that are billions of years old. Ridges and grooves in the lighter region indicate that when Ganymede was young, it was geologically active. Probably tectonic activity caused pieces of the icy crust to collide, causing fractures and furrows in the ice. Beneath the thick crust lies a mantle of ice and a rocky core.

Ganymede reveals large, dark regions of ancient craters and brighter areas of more recently developed ice in this *Voyager 1* image taken in March 1979 from 1.6 million miles (2.6 million km) away.

Callisto

Outermost of Jupiter's Galilean moons is Callisto. Like Ganymede, it's composed of rock and ice. But this pockmarked moon has no relatively smooth regions. Rather, it's completely overrun by craters. It actually is more densely cratered than any other object in the solar system. This indicates that Callisto has not experienced any tectonic activity or volcanism for a very long time. No lava flow has altered or filled in craters that were made by meteorites billions of years ago. Its largest impact basin, Valhalla, is 1,864 miles (3,000 km) wide—about half the diameter of Callisto itself.

This picture of crater-covered Callisto was taken by *Voyager 2* in July 1979 from a distance of 1.4 million miles (2.25 million km). The bright spots that cover Callisto are meteor impact craters.

Jupiter's ring system is illuminated by sunlight in this image taken by *Voyager 1*. The rings are shown in yellow, and the other two colors result from the filters used to take the image.

Jupiter's Rings

When *Voyager 1* reached Jupiter in 1979, scientists were especially interested in looking for rings. Saturn had rings, so perhaps Jupiter did, too. Sure enough, photographs revealed that Jupiter had a system of rings made up of tiny, dark particles. The largest ring, about 4,000 miles (6,500 km) wide, extends more than 35,000 miles (56,000 km) from Jupiter's cloud tops. Two other, thinner rings lie on either side of the main one and may have come from a small object that was pulled apart by gravitational forces.

This *Hubble Space Telescope* image of
Saturn clearly shows the divisions in its
ring system. Saturn is seen here at its
almost maximum tilt from Earth.

Saturn: Lord of the Rings

Four hundred years ago, when Galileo first peered at Saturn through his telescope, he noticed strange bulges, or handles, on either side of the planet. He announced to the world that Saturn was not a single planet but three. In 1655, Dutch astronomer Christian Huygens recognized the handles as rings. We had to wait more than 300 years before *Voyager* sent back our first up-close images of Saturn's splendid ring system.

The Romans named Saturn, the sixth planet from the Sun, after the father of Jupiter, the god of agriculture. It's the second-largest planet in the solar system, with a diameter of about 75,000 miles (120,000 km), nine times wider than Earth. If it were hollow, Saturn could contain 844 Earths. Like Jupiter, it rotates on its axis very rapidly, about once every 10.5 hours. Because it spins so quickly, Saturn bulges at the equator. In fact, its equatorial diameter is 7,500 miles (12,000 km) greater than the distance between its poles.

One complete orbit around the Sun takes 29.5 Earth years. During that orbit, we see Saturn and its rings from various angles, depending on the tilt of its axis. About every

This image illustrates the internal structure of Saturn. Moving inward from the exterior layer of molecular hydrogen, the pressure increases and hydrogen gas starts to resemble a hot liquid called metallic hydrogen. This metallic hydrogen state occurs at about half of Saturn's radius. Below this layer is a soupy liquid mixture of water, methane, and ammonia under high temperatures and pressure. Finally, at the center is a core of ice and rock.

seven and a half years, when Saturn appears to us straight on, the rings become almost invisible. The next time Saturn's rings will seem to disappear will be in September 2009.

Like the other gas giants, Saturn is composed primarily of hydrogen—about 96 percent. It also contains 3 percent helium, with traces of ammonia, methane, and water. A layer of metallic hydrogen surrounds its rocky, icy core. As on Jupiter, this layer creates a magnetic field. Although less powerful than Jupiter's, the field is 540 times as strong as Earth's. Above that layer is another of liquid hydrogen and helium. The temperature becomes steadily colder from the center out, ranging from 21,700°F (12,000°C) in the outer core to -301°F (-185°C) in the outer atmosphere. The cloudy atmosphere has three layers: a bottom layer of water ice and water vapor, a middle layer of ammonium hydrosulfide, and a top layer of ammonia ice crystals. A thick layer of hydrogen haze gives Saturn its characteristic butterscotch color.

Amazingly, despite its size, Saturn has only 70 percent the density of water, making it the least dense of all the planets. In fact, if there were a lake large enough to hold it, Saturn would float!

The Rings of Saturn

Saturn's ring system is the largest and most magnificent of all the planets. All together, the rings stretch across 260,000 miles (420,000 km), approximately the distance between Earth and the Moon. They are extremely thin, with a depth of only about 100 feet (30 m). The billions of ice particles that make up the rings range in size from small, dustlike grains to chunks as large as a house. Most are smaller than an inch (2.5 cm) across. Because they're made of ice, the particles are highly reflective, making Saturn's rings easily visible from Earth.

Using a telescope, we can see that the rings are divided into separate sections. But not until the *Voyager* missions could astronomers see their complex structure at close range. The rings are divided into seven main sections, which scientists have labeled A–G, and many of these have thousands of smaller ringlets. The two widest rings, B and A, are separated by a gap of 2,800 miles (4,500 km), called the Cassini Division.

The details of Saturn's rings are visible in this *Voyager* image. The colors were added by computer processing to show the ringlets more clearly.

The brightest and densest ring, B, is about 16,000 miles (25,500 km) wide and is solid enough to cast a slight shadow on Saturn.

Scientists theorize that the rings may have resulted when a larger body was torn apart by the forces of Saturn's gravity, or perhaps when two objects collided and were smashed into smaller pieces. As the debris orbited, these pieces kept crashing into one another, breaking up into ever smaller bits and gradually slowing down. Eventually, the cloud of particles flattened along Saturn's equator and formed a ring. There they were guided into separate paths by the gravitational pull of "shepherd" moons inside and outside the rings.

Saturn's Moons

Saturn has at least 30 known moons. The largest of these is Titan. With a diameter of 3,190 miles (5,150 km), Titan, like Jupiter's Ganymede, is larger than the planets Mercury and Pluto, making it the second-largest moon in the solar system. Like the large Galilean moons of Jupiter, it's composed of water ice and rock. Beneath the ice crust there may be a large body of water. What makes Titan unique is its thick atmosphere, which is 10 times thicker than Earth's. And like ours, Titan's is composed mainly of nitrogen. But instead of oxygen, it also contains methane, ethane, argon, hydrogen cyanide, and other compounds.

The imposing Herschel Crater extends over the face of Saturn's moon Mimas. It is an enormous impact crater with a raised rim and central peak.

We can't actually see Titan's surface, due to the thick layer of orange haze that blankets it entirely, but we know it is very cold, around -296°F (-182°C). Beneath the clouds, there may be methane seas and large, continent-like features. The near-infrared camera on the *Hubble Space Telescope* has sent back images of both bright and dark areas under the haze. One of the bright areas looks like a continent the size of Australia.

Many of Saturn's other moons were visible through Earth-based telescopes before the *Voyager* missions. But we had no idea how truly varied—and fascinating—the moons were. For instance, the innermost of Saturn's major moons, Mimas, is dominated by a mammoth crater named Herschel, which covers nearly one-third of the moon's surface. Scientists think that if the object that hit Mimas had been any larger, the moon would have totally shattered. When *Voyager* sent back the first images of Mimas in 1980, many observers noticed that it looked just like the Death Star in the movie *Star Wars*.

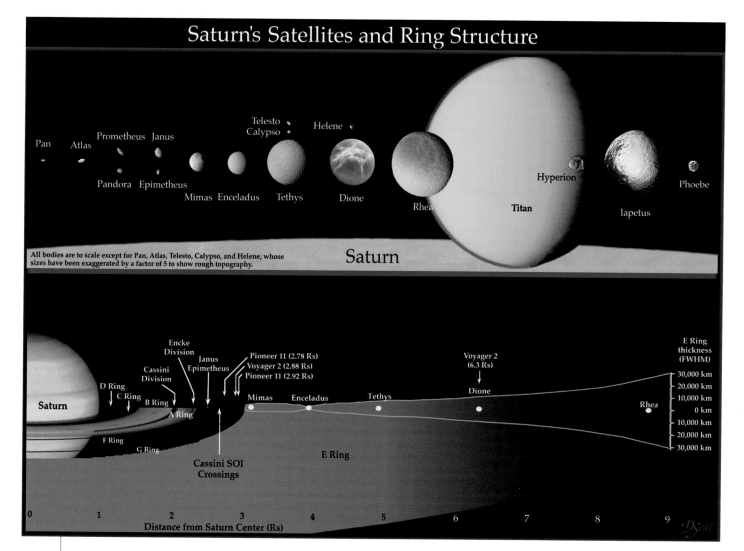

Saturn's Satellites and Ring Structure

All bodies are to scale except for Pan, Atlas, Telesto, Calypso, and Helene, whose sizes have been exaggerated by a factor of 5 to show rough topography.

Tethys is also heavily cratered. One crater, Odysseus, is larger than Mimas. A long canyon, the Ithaca Chasma, runs more than halfway around the moon. It was probably caused by tectonic activity below the icy crust.

Snow-white Enceladus is the brightest moon in the solar system. Much of its smooth, icy surface is reflective, broken only by ridges and faults. This ice, scientists think, must be quite recent, forming within the past 100 million years. It may have formed after internal heating caused water to break through to the surface and flow into the craters.

Both Dione and Rhea have patches of heavily cratered and relatively unbroken surfaces. Light streaks that cut across their surfaces may be cracks filled with ice.

An International Mission

The *Cassini* orbiter is the largest interplanetary spacecraft ever built. It's two stories tall and about 13 feet (4 m) wide. During its mission, it will send the equivalent of more than 400 CD-ROMs of information back to Earth, including more than 300,000 color images. The data will be analyzed by more than 200 scientists from 17 countries.

Strange Iapetus is two-faced: a bright cratered hemisphere on one side, a dark hemisphere on the other. Apparently Iapetus is coated in some mysterious dark material. It may be dust from Phoebe, the farthest moon from Saturn, which is also covered with some sort of dark substance. Or perhaps it is material that surges up from Iapetus's interior.

Many of the smallest moons are battered and misshapen. Some are probably parts of larger bodies that were shattered in a collision. Hyperion, 223 miles (360 km) wide, has been compared to a squashed hamburger.

Finally, there are the fascinating co-orbitals Janus and Epimetheus. Not only are these twin satellites about the same size, but also their orbits are only about 30 miles (48 km) apart. Every four years, the faster one overtakes the slower one. They exchange energy, and then they trade orbits. The faster one gets in the slow lane, and the slower one gets in the fast lane. In their synchronized orbits, Janus and Epimetheus look like speed skaters in a relay race.

In October 1997, NASA launched the *Cassini* spacecraft, which is scheduled to reach Saturn's orbit in June 2004. Once there, it will make roughly 30 orbits of the planet over four years and take at least 30,000 photographs. In particular, it will study the composition and geological history of Saturn's moons and the structure and origin of its rings. Scientists are especially impatient to identify the mysterious dark material on Iapetus's surface.

Perhaps most exciting, about four months into its orbit, *Cassini* will drop the *Huygens* probe into the thick atmosphere of Titan. During its two-and-a-half-hour descent, *Huygens* will measure the moon's atmosphere and take thousands of pictures. Then it will have just about 30 minutes—until its batteries give out—to send information from Titan's surface back to *Cassini*. Because Titan seems to contain some of the same chemicals that existed in Earth's early atmosphere, scientists hope the mission will tell them something about how life arose on our planet.

The spacecraft *Cassini* orbits Saturn in this artist's conception. Once it reaches Saturn, *Cassini* will spend four years studying the planet and its moons.

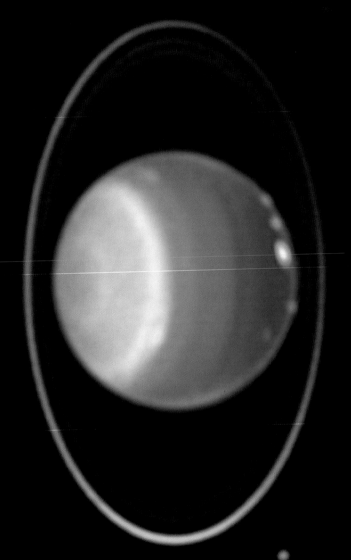

This 1998 *Hubble Space Telescope* false-color image shows Uranus surrounded by its rings and 10 of its satellites. Because Uranus's axis is tilted, its rings appear tilted, too.

Uranus: The Sideways Planet

The only gas giants observed and named by the ancient Greeks and Romans were Jupiter and Saturn. Uranus had to wait until 1781. On March 13, English astronomer William Herschel looked through his telescope and found a faint greenish disk. Though previous observers had thought it was a star, he realized that what he was seeing was a new planet. At first he wanted to call it "Georgium sidus" (the Georgian star), after King George III. But because all of the other planets had mythological names, the new planet was named Uranus, after the father of Saturn.

Uranus has a diameter of 31,800 miles (51,100 km), four times that of Earth, making it the third-largest planet in the solar system. A hollow Uranus could hold about 64 Earths. Because its mean distance from the Sun is 1.8 billion miles (2.9 billion km), Uranus takes 84 years to complete one revolution. It spins on its axis every 17 hours and 14 minutes.

What makes Uranus unique, however, is the topsy-turvy plane of its rotation. Other planets rotate in an upright, approximately perpendicular position. Uranus's axis of rotation, though, is tipped an extreme 98 degrees. As a result, Uranus spins on its side. For 42 years of its orbit, its north pole faces the Sun; then, for another 42 years, the south pole faces the Sun. Because of the axis's unusual inclination, scientists aren't absolutely sure which pole *is* the north pole. As with other planetary systems, Uranus's moons and rings are aligned along the plane of its equator. As a result, they appear tipped as well. How did

The interior of Uranus is composed of a rocky core and a mantle of water and icy gases, surrounded by a gaseous envelope of hydrogen, helium, and methane.

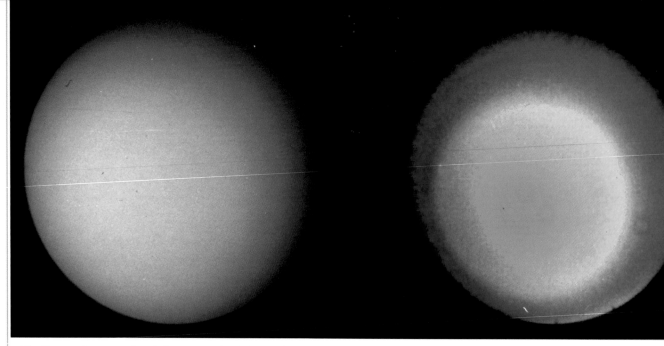

The *Voyager 2* spacecraft took these true-color (left) and false-color (right) images of Uranus from a range of 5.7 million miles (9.1 km). The false color in the image on the right depicts Uranus's polar regions. The uniform color of the left image reveals that Uranus has mild weather, compared to the other gas giants.

this happen? Experts think Uranus was probably hit by one or more large bodies in its youth and knocked over. But no one's quite sure.

Unlike Jupiter and Saturn, Uranus is composed primarily of rock and ice, with only about 15 percent hydrogen. Around its dense, rocky core lies a mantle of water ice, methane, and ammonia. Its cloudy atmosphere is about 83 percent hydrogen, 15 percent helium, and 2 percent methane and other trace elements. It's the methane in the top layer that gives the planet its soft aqua color, because methane absorbs red light.

Uranus's magnetic field is strong—much stronger than Earth's. Oddly, that field is offset from Uranus's axis of rotation by 60 degrees. This means that the magnetic poles lie closer to the equator than to the north and south geographic poles. What's more, the center of the magnetic field is not the center of the planet. The magnetic axes of other planets, including Earth, Jupiter, and Saturn, pass through almost their exact centers.

But on Uranus, the magnetic axis lies 4,800 miles (7,700 km) off center. Scientists think that Uranus's magnetic field is generated in the mantle, far from the planet's core, where interior seas of water and ammonia conduct electricity.

When *Voyager 2* visited Uranus in 1986, the layers of hazy clouds made it seem almost featureless. More recent *Hubble Space Telescope* observations have revealed bright clouds and the possibility of weather. Winds at middle latitudes have been measured at up to 375 miles (600 km) per hour. It seems that the Uranian atmosphere isn't so calm after all.

Before *Voyager 2* was launched, astronomers already knew that Uranus had rings. In March 1977, observers watched as the planet passed in front of a star. Even before Uranus reached the star, the star's light

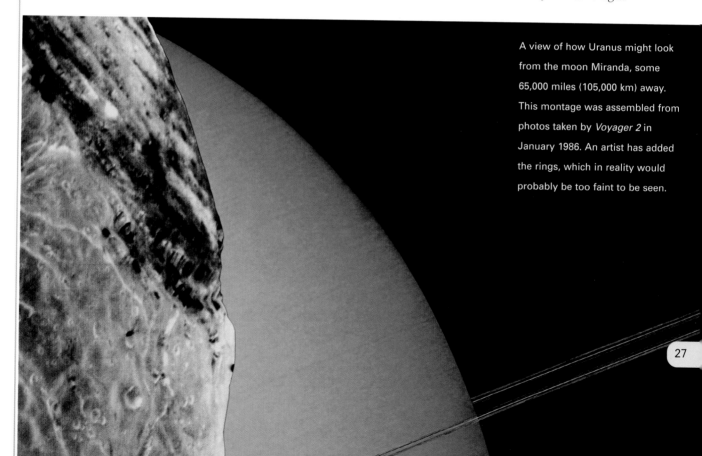

A view of how Uranus might look from the moon Miranda, some 65,000 miles (105,000 km) away. This montage was assembled from photos taken by *Voyager 2* in January 1986. An artist has added the rings, which in reality would probably be too faint to be seen.

dimmed, brightened, and then dimmed again. After Uranus had passed, this pattern repeated itself. Astronomers couldn't see the rings directly, but they knew the rings had to be there. *Voyager 2* confirmed that Uranus does indeed have 11 very thin rings. At 62 miles (100 km) wide, the outer ring, Epsilon, is the largest. It's kept in its orbit by two shepherd moons, Cordelia and Ophelia. The rings are made of dark particles ranging from fine dust to bodies up to 33 feet (10 m) wide.

Most solar system moons have names taken from classical mythology. However, Uranus's moons are named after characters from the plays of William Shakespeare and the poem *The Rape of the Lock* by Alexander Pope. The five largest moons were known before the trip of *Voyager 2*. Herschel sighted the two largest, Titania and Oberon, in 1787. *Voyager 2* discovered 10 small, dark inner ones, and 6 more distant moons have been sighted since. They're all quite small, ranging from 963 miles (1,550 km) down to 19 miles (30 km) in diameter.

One of the most fascinating is Miranda, which is only about 300 miles (480 km) in diameter. From a distance it looks as if someone has taken a giant knife and scraped long parallel grooves in its rocky surface. One feature looks like a giant check mark, while another looks like an oval racing track. One canyon is 9 miles (15 km) deep, about 10 times deeper than the Grand Canyon on Earth. Scientists have debated how Miranda might have ended up looking so bizarre. One possibility is that it broke into separate pieces when it collided with an asteroid or comet. When the chunks stuck together again, they formed the strange patchwork of features we see today.

This montage of the Uranian system, prepared from images taken by *Voyager 2*, shows Uranus's six largest moons. In this artist's view, Ariel is in the foreground. Clockwise from Ariel are the satellites Umbriel, Oberon, Titania, Miranda, and the small moon Puck, which is only 95 miles (150 km) in diameter.

Neptune is seen over Triton's horizon in this *Voyager 2* photo.

CHAPTER FOUR

Neptune: The Dynamic Planet

Astronomers observing Uranus in the early 1800s noticed that the planet was not always where their mathematical tables said it should be. Perhaps, they thought, there was another unknown body nearby whose gravity was tugging at Uranus.

Astronomers John Couch Adams in England and Urbain Leverrier in France both decided to investigate the possibility of another, unknown planet. Working independently, they each calculated the hypothetical planet's position in the heavens. On September 23, 1846, when German astronomer Johann Gottfried Galle received Leverrier's calculations, he turned his telescope toward the area of the sky where the new planet was supposed to be. That very night he saw a faint light where no star existed. The new planet was named Neptune, after the Roman god of the seas.

Neptune is so far from Earth—2.6 billion miles (4.2 billion km) is the nearest it ever comes—that astronomers knew relatively little about it until *Voyager 2* arrived in 1989, twelve years after its launch. *Voyager 2* passed closer to Neptune than to the other gas giants, only 2,700 miles (4,400 km) above its north pole. Neptune, astronomers thought, would be a quiet planet, like Uranus. To their surprise, they discovered that in some ways it was more like Jupiter—active, turbulent, and changeable.

The eighth planet has a diameter of 30,800 miles (49,500 km), about four times wider than Earth's. If Neptune were hollow, it could hold nearly 60 Earths. At an average distance of 2.8 billion miles (4.5 billion km) from the Sun, Neptune is frigid indeed, about -360°F (-218°C) in its upper atmosphere. This is cold enough to freeze methane. It's no wonder that the planet is so cold—Neptune receives 900 times less sunlight than Earth. Because it is so far away, Neptune takes a long time, 165 years, to complete one revolution around the Sun. On June 8, 2011, it will complete its first full orbit since its discovery in 1846. Sometimes Pluto's highly elliptical orbit crosses the orbit of Neptune. Then, for a few years, Neptune is not the eighth planet from the Sun, but the ninth.

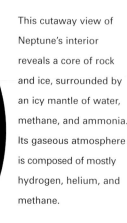

This cutaway view of Neptune's interior reveals a core of rock and ice, surrounded by an icy mantle of water, methane, and ammonia. Its gaseous atmosphere is composed of mostly hydrogen, helium, and methane.

At the center of the planet lies a core of melted silicate rock, surrounded by a mantle of water, ammonia, and methane ice. Like Uranus, Neptune has a magnetic axis that is out of alignment with its rotational axis. Also like Uranus, it has a magnetic field that is probably generated by the liquid in its middle layer, rather than in its core.

Neptune's atmosphere is 80 percent hydrogen, 19 percent helium, 1 percent methane, and a mixture of other trace gases. Its rich blue color comes from the methane and probably another unidentified compound in its upper atmosphere. Heat rising from the hot interior creates stormy weather in the cloud layers, where fierce winds reach up to 1,500 miles (2,400 km) per hour. These are the fastest winds in the solar system.

When *Voyager 2* flew by Neptune, the planet's most prominent feature was a huge storm in the southern hemisphere called the Great Dark Spot. It was about half the size of Jupiter's Great

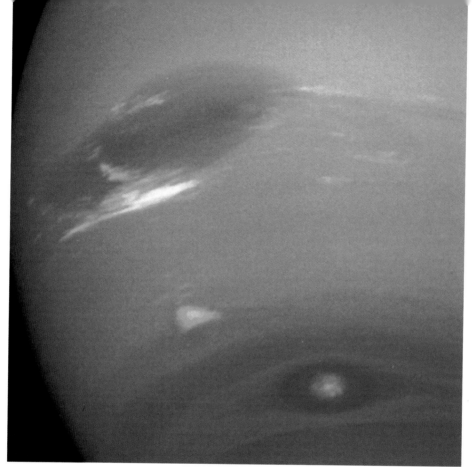

The Great Dark Spot, here seen from *Voyager 2*, is a huge storm system in Neptune's turbulent atmosphere. Midway between the Great Dark Spot and the Small Dark Spot beneath it is a white cloud patch nicknamed Scooter that zips around the planet.

Red Spot. *Voyager 2* also spotted another possible storm, a small white cloud called Scooter, that breezed around the planet about every 16 hours.

Five years later, when the *Hubble Space Telescope* was turned toward Neptune, the Great Dark Spot had disappeared, and a smaller, dark storm had appeared in the northern hemisphere. Apparently, Neptune's atmosphere changes very rapidly indeed.

Like Uranus, Neptune has rings of dark particles, with some denser clumps called ring arcs. The closest ring is about 26,000 (42,000 km) from the planet; the farthest is about 39,000 miles (63,000 km) away. The rings were named after the planet's discoverers: Adams, Leverrier, and Galle.

33

Just a few weeks after Galle got his first glimpse of Neptune, British astronomer William Lassell discovered Neptune's largest moon. It was named Triton, after Neptune's son. Ten more moons have since been discovered, three very recently. Triton has a diameter of 1,680 miles (2,700 km); all of the others are 261 miles (420 km) or less in diameter.

Triton is peculiar in a number of ways. For one thing, its orbit is both very elliptical and retrograde. That means it moves around Neptune in the direction opposite to Neptune's rotation and that of the other satellites. Astronomers think that perhaps Triton was once an independent body that was captured by Neptune's gravity.

Also, with a surface temperature of ⁻391°F (⁻235°C), Triton is one of the coldest known places in the solar system. Through its surface of nitrogen and methane ice, geysers of nitrogen gas shoot five miles (8 km) into the air. Dust carried by the geysers leaves dark streaks across the icy terrain. At the polar caps, the ice appears slightly pink, possibly because of organic compounds. Around the equator, the surface is bumpy and pitted. Scientists call this a cantaloupe terrain because it looks a lot like melon skin. Frozen Triton, scientists think, may be a lot like the ninth planet, Pluto.

Message to the Universe

When *Voyager 2* completed its flyby of Neptune in 1989 and headed out to the stars, it carried a message from Earth to the universe. Attached to the side of each *Voyager* spacecraft is a 12-inch (30.5 cm) gold phonograph record with sounds and images representative of life on Earth. It contains natural sounds, such as waves breaking on a shore, a baby crying, crickets chirping, and birds singing, as well as human sounds, such as Eastern and Western music. It also contains greetings from people on Earth in 55 different languages. Encoded in the disk is a diagram showing what humans look like and where Earth is in the solar system. We don't know whether, in their intersteller wanderings, *Voyager 1* and *2* will ever encounter an advanced civilization. But maybe, someday, an alien will listen to a whale song and wonder what it is. . . .

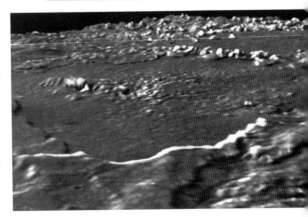

Voyager 2 images taken on August 24, 1989, were used to create this computerized perspective of the surface of Triton.

Many scientists consider Triton to be the
most beautiful moon in the solar system.
At the south pole it is covered by a pinkish
ice cap. Closer to the equator, its surface is
bumpy and pitted, like cantaloupe skin. In
this computer-generated montage, Neptune
appears in the background.

Pluto: A World of Rock and Ice

The discovery of Pluto resulted from some very lucky detective work. In the early 20th century, some astronomers saw inconsistencies in the orbits of Uranus and Neptune and thought another planet might be to blame. For 25 years, observers searched the skies. Finally, on February 18, 1930, a young astronomer named Clyde Tombaugh was looking at a pair

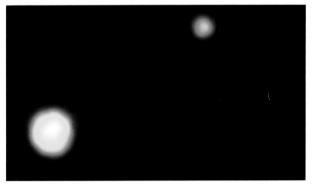

This is the clearest view we have of the planet Pluto and its moon Charon, as seen through the *Hubble Space Telescope*. The image was taken on February 21, 1994, when the planet was 2.6 billion miles (4.4 billion km) from Earth. In Earth-based telescopes, the two images appear blurred together.

of photographs of the night sky when he saw one tiny spot of light change position against the background of the fixed stars. He knew immediately it must be Planet X. The new planet was dubbed Pluto, after the Roman god of the underworld. Ironically, it turned out that Pluto was far too small to interfere with the orbits of the gas giants after all.

Clyde Tombaugh, the discoverer of Pluto, peers through a telescope at the Lowell Observatory in Flagstaff, Arizona.

37

The most distant and smallest of the planets, Pluto is an average distance of 3.7 billion miles (6 billion km) from the Sun. With a diameter of 1,440 miles (2,320 km), it's also smaller than all four of Jupiter's Galilean moons, Titan, Triton, and our Moon. It's so distant that one revolution of the Sun takes 248 years. Pluto's orbit is highly elliptical, or oval, so for two 20-year periods during its orbit, it is actually closer to the Sun than Neptune is. One of those 20-year periods was from January 21, 1979, through February 11, 1999.

Like Uranus, Pluto is tipped sideways. Its axis is steeply tilted to about 123 degrees, so its north pole is below the plane of its orbit. As if that wasn't eccentric enough, it also rotates in the direction opposite that of most of the other planets, just as Triton does.

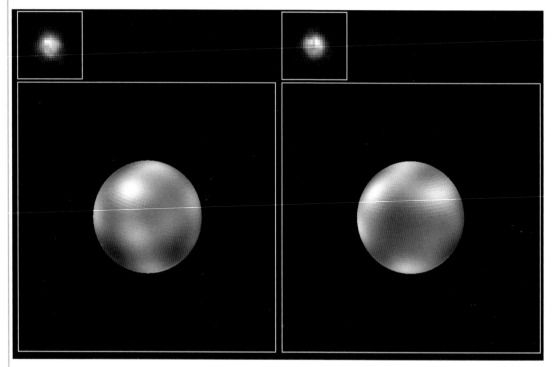

These are images of the never-before-seen surface of the planet Pluto, as revealed by the *Hubble Space Telescope*. In the small inset pictures at the top—the actual *Hubble* images—each square pixel is 100 miles (160 km) across. The larger images at the bottom, constructed through computer imaging processing, show dramatic contrast between light and dark areas on Pluto's surface. Opposite hemispheres of Pluto are seen in these two views.

Pluto is so far away that it can be seen only through the largest telescope on Earth. Even the *Hubble Space Telescope* can only dimly make out some of its features. The *Hubble* has shown us that Pluto has areas as dark as coal and as white as snow. Because Pluto is the only planet never to have been visited by spacecraft, we can only make informed conjectures about its geology and composition.

Scientists think that Pluto's surface is covered with nitrogen and methane ice, just like Triton's. Under an interior layer of water ice, there is a very large rocky core. When Pluto is closest to the Sun, some of the ice evaporates to form an extremely thin atmosphere of nitrogen, carbon dioxide, and methane. Then the planet may warm to -410°F (-246°C), only to drop back to -391°F (-235°C) when it spins farther from the Sun.

The parallels between the orbits and compositions of Pluto and Triton have led scientists to surmise that they might have similar histories. Perhaps they were formed in the same part of the early solar nebula with other like objects. Triton was captured by Neptune, while Pluto remained independent. Other similar bodies might have become comets in the Oort cloud of comets that lies beyond Pluto's orbit.

Some scientists question whether Pluto is a planet at all. They note its small size and greater similarity to comets than to the other planets. On the other hand, Pluto *is* orbiting the Sun, not another planet. And most important, Pluto has its own moon, Charon, which was discovered in 1978. In Greek and Roman mythology, Charon is the boatman who ferries the dead across the River Styx into Hades, where Pluto rules.

New Moon

Like so many astronomical discoveries, the sighting of Pluto's moon Charon was an accident. On the afternoon of June 22, 1978, astronomer Jim Christy was hard at work at the U.S. Naval Observatory, measuring Pluto's orbit on a set of photographic plates. In some of the images Pluto looked strange and elongated, as if it were attached to a smaller white blob. Perhaps there was a defect in the plates, Christy thought. But the stars surrounding Pluto looked perfect. The blob was too tall to be a mountain, and too steady to be a volcanic eruption. Could it be that Pluto had a moon?

Excited, Christy calculated that the orbit of the moon was exactly synchronized to Pluto's rotation period. He had made astronomical history. The discovery of Charon was announced on July 8, 1978.

Charon is 790 miles (1,270 km) in diameter, about half the diameter of Pluto. That makes it the largest moon in relation to its planet in the solar system. Many scientists think of the two as a double planet. There are two theories about Charon's creation. One is that, like Pluto, it was once an independent body. When the two were caught in the pull of each other's gravity, they became a double planet system. The other theory is that another object slammed into Pluto, and the mantles of both objects blew off into space. The debris coalesced to form Charon.

Scientists think that Charon is covered by water ice, unlike Pluto, which is covered by methane frost. Otherwise, its composition is thought to be about the same as Pluto's and Triton's: about 75 percent rock and 25 percent water ice.

Charon is 11,400 miles (18,400 km) from Pluto. Like Pluto, it spins on its axis every 6.4 days. As it happens, Charon also orbits Pluto every 6.4 days. Because Charon's orbit is synchronous with both its rotation and Pluto's, they always keep the same faces toward each other. Observers standing on Charon's near side would see Pluto at all times. From the far side, they would never see Pluto at all.

Their codependency goes even farther. It's possible that they share the same atmosphere during the short period when Pluto has an atmosphere. Even more amazing, they probably share the same center of gravity. In most planet-moon systems, the center of gravity is close to the center of the planet. But the masses of Charon and Pluto are so close that their center of gravity is located outside their bodies and in the space between them. They circle this imaginary line in their orbit around the Sun.

NASA is hoping to launch the Pluto-Kuiper Belt Mission in 2006. The goal of the mission will be to send a spacecraft by Pluto and Charon in 2015 which will then go on to investigate the Kuiper belt objects, icy chunks orbiting beyond Neptune. The mission will give us the opportunity to learn more about the fascinating worlds at the edge of our solar system.

In this artist's conception, the *Pluto-Kuiper Express* spacecraft arrives at Pluto in about the year 2015. The spacecraft will pass within 9,300 miles (15,000 km) of Pluto and Charon.

41

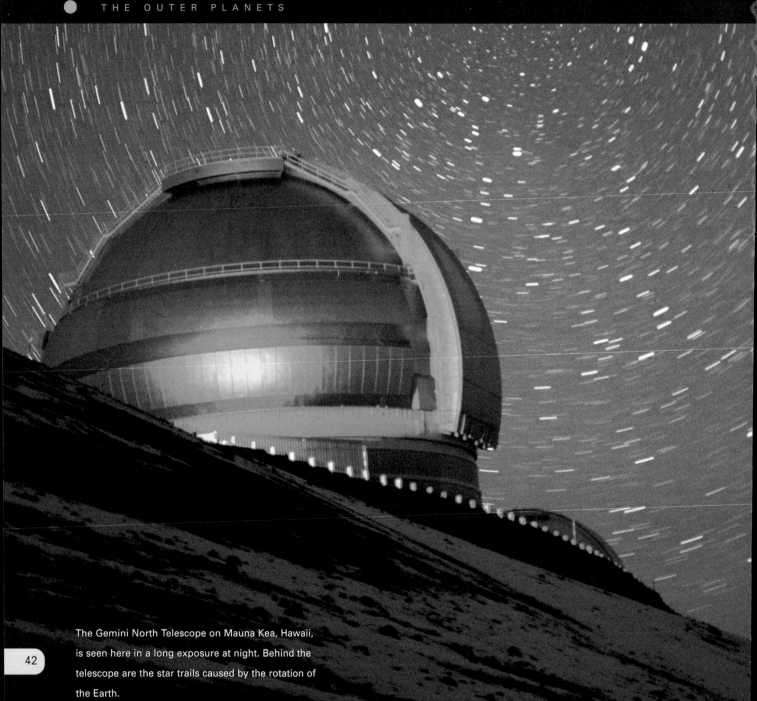

The Gemini North Telescope on Mauna Kea, Hawaii, is seen here in a long exposure at night. Behind the telescope are the star trails caused by the rotation of the Earth.

Observing Distant Worlds

From the perspective of Earth, the planets move across the night sky within a band of stars that the ancient Greeks called the zodiac. There are 12 constellations, or star groups, in the zodiac, and planets travel through all of them during one revolution around the Sun. To observe a planet, locate it within the constellation it is in for that month. You can also find out where it is by consulting an almanac or a newspaper or by looking at monthly sky charts on the Internet. (Some addresses are listed in the back of this book.) Sky charts also can be found in magazines such as *Astronomy* and *Sky & Telescope*.

Of the giant gas planets, only Jupiter and Saturn are readily observable with the naked eye. Once they become familiar, it's not difficult to tell these planets apart from stars. Stars twinkle as their light passes through Earth's atmosphere. Planets, much closer to us than stars, shine more steadily. They look like flat disks in the reflected light of the Sun.

Jupiter and Saturn can be seen more clearly with binoculars. But in order to see any detail in these planets—or to locate the other planets at all—you will need a telescope. If you don't have one, check out a planetarium in a local college or a science museum in your area. In addition to sky shows, lectures, and courses, planetariums often have observing sessions when visitors can look through their telescopes. Local astronomy clubs also offer special viewing sessions for the public.

The best time to see any of the outer planets is when they are in opposition—that is, opposite the Sun in the sky. Not only do they then look brighter and larger, but they are also visible all night.

Here's what you can expect when the outer planets are observed.

Jupiter

Jupiter is very bright—the second-brightest planet after Venus and three times as bright as the brightest star, Sirius. Through binoculars, it looks like a disk. If you know what you're looking for, you can also spot the four Galilean moons on a clear night. They look like very faint points of light.

With a small telescope, you should be able to make out the cloud belts and zones that lie along Jupiter's equator. The Galilean moons will be lined up along the planet's equatorial plane. If you can't see one of the four, it's because the moon is either behind or in front of Jupiter.

Jupiter is in opposition every 13 months. You can check a sky chart to see what constellation Jupiter lies in during any month.

Saturn

Saturn can be seen with binoculars as a flat disk. Its rings, however, will not be visible. With a small telescope, you can see them distinctly. On particularly clear nights, you might even be able to make out the Cassini Division, the largest space between the rings. During Saturn's 29.5-year orbit of the Sun, its rings will appear to be at different angles. At most, they are tilted toward Earth about 27 degrees. Twice in its orbit, the rings will appear straight on and be nearly invisible. This will happen next in September 2009.

A medium-sized telescope will reveal Saturn's moons, especially the largest, Titan. They orbit along the plane of Saturn's equator.

Saturn is in opposition once every year and two weeks.

Uranus

Uranus can be located with the naked eye when it is in opposition, but only if you know exactly where to look. With the use of a star chart, you can find it with a pair of binoculars or a small telescope. It appears as a small greenish disk.

Uranus is in opposition every year and four days. Between 2003 and 2009, it will be passing through the constellations Aquarius and Pisces.

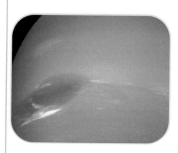

Neptune

At an average of 2.7 billion miles (4.4 billion km) from Earth, Neptune is invisible to the naked eye. Even if you use binoculars, it's so faint that you have to be a proficient sky-gazer to be able to see it. With a telescope, you'll see it as a small bluish disk.

Between 2003 and 2009, it will be passing through the constellations Capricorn and Aquarius. It is in opposition every year and two and a half days.

Pluto

Pluto is visible only with a large telescope. Even then, the small point of light you'll see will be Pluto and Charon together. Because Pluto's orbit is inclined 17.2 degrees, it can't be seen along the ecliptic plane as the other planets can. Between 2003 and 2009, it will pass through the constellations Ophiuchus and Serpens Cauda, above Sagittarius.

Further Information

Apfel, Necia H. *Voyager to the Planets*. New York: Clarion Books, 1991.

Cole, Michael D. *Saturn: the Sixth Planet*. Berkeley Heights, New Jersey: Enslow Publishers, 2002.

Haugen, David M. *Jupiter*. San Diego: Kidhaven Press, 2002.

Kerrod, Robin. *Jupiter*. Minneapolis: Lerner Books, 2000.

Kerrod, Robin. *Saturn*. Minneapolis: Lerner Books, 2000.

Kerrod, Robin. *Uranus, Neptune, and Pluto*. Minneapolis: Lerner Books, 2000.

Mitton, Simon and Jacqueline Mitton. *The Young Oxford Book of Astronomy*. New York: Oxford University Press, 1995.

Vogt, Gregory L. *Jupiter, Saturn, Uranus, and Neptune*. Chatham, New Jersey: Raintree Steck-Vaughn, 2000.

"Nine Planets" by Bill Arnett. October 2000. Up-to-date information on each of the planets. http://seds.lpl.arizona.edu/nineplanets/nineplanets/nineplanets.html

NASA's official Web site on the *Galileo* space mission. www.jpl.nasa.gov.galileo

NASA's Web site for kids. kids.msfc.nasa.gov

The basics of backyard astronomy. www.mindspring.com/community/featrepgs/astronomy98/

Information on the Pluto–Kuiper Belt Mission. pluto.jhuapl.edu/mission.htm

Cassini-Huygens Mission to Saturn and Titan. saturn.jpl.nasa.gov/cassini/index.shtml

Sky charts and information for backyard astronomy. www.skyandtelescope.com

Excellent site on backyard astronomy, including sky calendar. www.space.com/spacewatch/

Glossary

aphelion—The point in its orbit at which a planet is farthest from the Sun.

axis of rotation—The imaginary line running through an object around which it spins. Also known as the poles.

comet—A gigantic ball of ice, dust, and rock that orbits the Sun in a highly eccentric orbit. Some comets have an orbit that brings them close to the Sun, where they form a long tail of gas and dust as they are heated by the Sun's rays.

constellation—Points of stars that early stargazers connected to make imaginary pictures in the night sky. There are 88 constellations.

ecliptic—An imaginary line in the sky traced by Earth as it moves one full revolution around the Sun.

elliptical—To be shaped in an ellipse (oval). Johannes Kepler discovered that the orbits of the planets were elliptical in shape rather than circular.

flyby—A space mission that passes close enough to observe the Sun, a planet, moon, asteroid, or comet.

Galilean moons—The name given to Jupiter's four largest moons: Io, Europa, Callisto, and Ganymede. They were discovered independently by Galileo Galilei and Simon Marius.

gravity—A force associated with bodies in motion in which a rotating object creates a force of attraction.

gravity assist—Using a planet or moon's gravity to help a spacecraft accelerate or slow down.

impact crater—A crater formed when a smaller cosmic body, such as a meteorite, strikes a larger body, such as a planet.

magnetic field—An area of magnetic influence that circulates between the two poles of a magnet.

magnetosphere—A magnetic field that envelopes a planet, flowing between the north pole and the south pole. The magnetosphere helps protect planets from harmful cosmic influences.

mantle—The interior of a planet that lies between the crust and the central core.

mass—A quantity or aggregate of matter.

meteor—A streak of light, often called a "falling" or "shooting" star, produced when a sand- or gravel-sized grain of interplanetary material plunges into Earth's atmosphere and glows from the heat of friction with air molecules.

moon—An object that is caught in the gravitational influence of a larger body and orbits it.

nebula—A diffuse mass of interstellar dust and gas.

opposition—The position of a planet when it is exactly opposite the Sun as seen from Earth.

orbit—The path of an object through space as it travels around another object with greater mass.

perihelion—The point in its orbit at which a planet is closest to the Sun.

planetesimal—Matter formed when our solar system was born. Colliding planetesimals probably collected and formed the planets. Asteroids and comets are leftover planetesimals.

probe—An unmanned spacecraft used to explore the solar system that sends its data back to Earth.

radiation—Energy that travels via electromagnetic waves. Some radiation is dangerous; some is not. Radiation from the Sun provides heat and light. Radiation from x-rays can damage tissue.

retrograde motion—Having a direction that is contrary to the general motion of similar bodies.

terrestrial planet—One of the four rocky, or inner, planets in the solar system.

tidal force—The gravitational pull on planetary objects from nearby planets and moons.

zodiac—An imaginary belt across the sky in which the Sun, Moon, and all the planets except Pluto can always be found.

Index

48